T0209439

Spark

Statements of Truth During Pregnancy and Beyond

Kathy Grissom

BALBOA.
PRESS
A DIVISION OF HAY HOUSE

This book is a work of non-fiction. Unless otherwise noted, the author and the publisher make no explicit guarantees as to the accuracy of the information contained in this book and in some cases, names of people and places have been altered to protect their privacy.

Balboa Press books may be ordered through booksellers or by contacting:

Balboa Press
A Division of Hay House
1663 Liberty Drive
Bloomington, IN 47403
www.balboapress.com
1 (877) 407-4847

Because of the dynamic nature of the Internet, any web addresses or links contained in this book may have changed since publication and may no longer be valid. The views expressed in this work are solely those of the author and do not necessarily reflect the views of the publisher, and the publisher hereby disclaims any responsibility for them.

The author of this book does not dispense medical advice or prescribe the use of any technique as a form of treatment for physical, emotional, or medical problems without the advice of a physician, either directly or indirectly. The intent of the author is only to offer information of a general nature to help you in your quest for emotional and spiritual well-being. In the event you use any of the information in this book for yourself, which is your constitutional right, the author and the publisher assume no responsibility for your actions.

Any people depicted in stock imagery provided by Getty Images are models, and such images are being used for illustrative purposes only.
Certain stock imagery © Getty Images.

Print information available on the last page.

ISBN: 978-1-9822-1874-4 (sc)
ISBN: 978-1-9822-1876-8 (hc)
ISBN: 978-1-9822-1875-1 (e)

Library of Congress Control Number: 2019908146

Balboa Press rev. date: 06/24/2019

Acknowledgments

I would like to dedicate this book to all the children of the world, praying for peace, love and harmony among every new generation that comes forward.

A very special thanks to a dear friend Reamie Tabin for the photography and for years of inspiring conversations, as well as growing through Reiki classes together. To Angelina Bailey a young aspiring artist for the cover artwork that is amazingly brilliant, who is also the niece of Reamie.

Many family members and friends play an inspirational role in my life. I give love and thanks to everyone for supporting me on this journey. Jackie and Pam are lifelong friends that I am so blessed to have such enduring friendships.

To my sons Eric and Brett, who are my biggest supporters, and who are loved to the moon and back, and to Emerald for being a positive contribution to our family. My husband Don has encouraged me to grow and find my true self, for that I am very grateful. Also, to my sisters Janet and Linda and my brother John for their never-ending love and support at every crossroad in my life; and being my biggest fans.

As always, I am so grateful for the abundance in my life on so many levels. I continue to bless and give thanks for the completion of this project and look forward to the birth of the next.

I wish you love, peace and joy forever more.

As the responsible woman you are, now carrying a child within you, first let me congratulate you on your pregnancy. You are wise to begin this book for you and your child. It doesn't matter how far along you are into your pregnancy when you begin reading it. I wrote this book to strengthen you and your child physically, mentally, and spiritually, hoping it will nurture a healthy mind-set for both of you. All the work you put into your pregnancy with true, positive thoughts will be rewarded.

I am a Reiki master. Therefore, I am a firm believer in the power of the energy we have within us. However, this book is not about Reiki or religion; it's about believing in your own power or faith. It's about the hope you exude, for when you have hope, you have faith and you believe.

This is your superpower in believing, so put your faith into a mission to leave your legacy as a woman who wants to do something big, to be part of a oneness that is so big that it changes the world into a better place, one child at a time. I hope these statements of truth are helpful as well as inspiring so it brings your awareness to such clarity that you enrich your child from the point of conception. As my niece Ashley says, "Let love lead."

It has been my experience that as you focus upon what you do want and stay in that positive mind-set, more of the same comes to you, which is often called manifesting your dreams or desires. However, what people fail to do is believe. I believe wholeheartedly that this book will enrich your experience of pregnancy. The connection is made instantaneously because the baby can feel your emotional vibrations.

Just as you walk into a room and feel uneasy or safe, your emotional vibration invokes your senses. This is how you communicate with your child while pregnant. I feel my way through life. I feel joy and I receive joy. I feel at ease with my child, and my child is at ease. When I tense up, so does my child. Connection vibrationally is like a soul-to-soul connection.

It is important to take a few minutes each day to read your daily statements of truth; but if you miss one day, don't get discouraged—just pick up where you left off and continue on your journey. Every pregnancy is different because every new little soul within you is different yet still connected to the oneness of the universe.

Every human being is conceived by the energy spark of life. It's the moment when God, or source energy, breathes life into the embryo and produces a perfect image from God's imagination. All is perfect with the baby you conceive and give birth to. Every child is special; every child is unique; every child represents the love of the universe. This is a soul delivered to you. Nothing is more pure or natural.

Your child feels your emotions and can interpret your thoughts through feelings. Therefore, when you are happy, that positive energy is a vibrational match to your child because your child knows nothing less than pure, positive energy at this point of development. However, your less-than-joyful feelings also vibrate messages to your child. Therefore, try your best to be your best every single day. Stay present in the moment and take note of how you feel throughout the day.

Remember to take time for yourself to meditate and quiet your mind each day. The way you do this is by first connecting to God/source energy and then connecting your God/source energy with that of your unborn child's. When you can find that quiet space, you are connected, and in that state, you can tune into your thoughts of pure love and admiration for your child.

If we believe that we create our own realities by thinking intentional thoughts and feeling emotions, then it stands to reason that we can think big for our children. We can influence them from within the womb to think and feel the purest thoughts in order to gain their best lives possible. We can reach for thoughts of a harmonious, peaceful existence by always choosing to align with our inner higher selves. We can teach them through our own practice to quiet the mind and look for inner strength as a path that will bring clarity and happiness during their lifetimes. We can teach our children to rely on their own inner compasses, which is what we call intuition.

My dream for this world is for the women, mothers of children, to take the lead toward peace and harmony, planting the seeds of a desire for excellence within each child, raising this new generation of children to enhance change to the world for the better, allowing them to feel the connection of spiritual consciousness within the womb and beyond and to come into this world with a sense of positive energy. Let's let them know and feel what is right so they can stay tuned into a nonviolent approach to living a better life. Our physical existence in this world is for growing, expanding, and becoming enlightened during our lifetimes to cocreate experiences that enhance our physical lives. What if we can bear children who recognize enlightenment from birth and use their minds to heal, empowering all children to heal themselves and heal our planet? Women of every country, nationality, and spiritual origin can contribute to the world by doing their part in bearing children with purpose, integrity, and higher consciousness. What a beautiful gift to the world!

Much work needs to be done. Let's get started so you can be truly connected to God/source energy when manifestation takes place; with mothers joining it will be your legacy to parent children with kindness and compassion. Fill your cup first with positive energy and let the overflowing energy reach far and wide to create an abundance that feeds the world in unmeasurable greatness. It all starts with just one person's vision. I intend to make my purpose in life to be a bright shining light of encouragement. And so it is.

You may be pregnant for a few weeks before it is confirmed, so I don't want you to think it is too late to start reading and practicing statements of truth over your baby and yourself. If you pick this book up before you are pregnant, then that is wonderful. Or if you're a couple of months pregnant, then that is wonderful as well. You see, however or whenever you start, it is all divine timing and is the perfect time. Just begin and keep using these statements of truth until the child is born. It's not the schedule that matters but the connection you build as a liaison between God/source energy and extending that positive influence to include your child—such a beautiful gift to yourself, your child, and the world! Each one of us is an extension of source energy, including the child you are now carrying.

This book references *statements of truth* because your truth is your power. Where there is balance and harmony, there is also joy. The purpose of life for me is to simply enjoy and explore existence in a state of mindfulness because that will inspire new ideas and desires, which is the foundation of expansion or growth of a person. So simply practice mindfulness to be always striving for the better feelings; that is when the magic will happen— things will manifest in your life that flow with ease and grace. You are not pushing anything; it just happens naturally.

It's time to prepare for the most exciting time of your life. You have been blessed, and I know you are ready!

The book is broken down into weekly and daily call and responses with your child. It will serve as a daily meditation connection soul to soul. Think of it as a direct nonphysical channel to communicate vibrationally or verbally, opening the access to mindfulness and focus positive thoughts toward this little soul. I believe that through prayer and speaking positive words over a child will create a higher expectation toward always choosing love in life.

The daily statements of truth are for you and your child. It will inspire thoughts and further dialogue if you wish. New thoughts may enter your mind, and that is natural. It would be nice to take at least fifteen minutes to meditate on the intention of the statement of truth. Quiet your mind to say the statement of truth and then relax and feel what thoughts or images come to mind. Try to get past those thoughts and images to nothingness. When you get there, you are connected to your God/source energy. You will feel it. You'll sense calmness, and then maybe an inspiration will suddenly come into your mind. Allow and follow that inspiration, for that is your personal message. You might want to keep a journal and write down your thoughts or feelings; whatever works best for you is most important. The point is to remain mindful of these thoughts of inspiration after your fifteen minutes of mediation/prayer.

However, if you are a busy mother-to-be and cannot spend fifteen minutes, then just read the statement of truth and close your eyes for one minute, holding that thought. This can also be very powerful over the course of nine months. Please be kind to yourself and don't worry that you are doing anything wrong, for the beauty of this book is to make it your own personal journey.

When speaking statements of truth, you are confirming your thoughts and words to God/source energy and are declaring a truth for you and your baby. I like to believe that your words are your wand. By speaking a truth that is true and believable to you, it then is without convictions that you stand totally in alignment with what you are speaking. This vibrational force is so strong that you will see evidence in your daily routine that things just flow effortlessly. When you speak good things, it amplifies your words to the universe and to your baby. Therefore, it naturally returns to you in ways of kindness from a stranger, finding the missing item you were looking for, or even a sale on something you need. The focus is to believe in what you are doing and have faith to trust the process, for it works. Speaking your words into reality is creating your own reality because you will always get back what you give out. Your intention of your words must be pure and genuine for the best results.

I want to be perfectly clear that we are not trying to change the baby. Your baby is a beautiful gift. The purpose is to enhance the experience for you and your baby by vibrating positively and staying in harmony with your inner soul. We can influence another being, but we do not have the ability to change anyone. Each person who comes forth into this world as an extension of God is perfect. Your baby will develop and become who he or she is by making choices from their own free will. A baby's soul comes forth filled with the purest love. Every choice you make will influence your child with positive or negative emotions.

I am sure you are ready to begin, so turn the page and enjoy the experience that you will cocreate. Love is the foundation of this manifestation—and may you feel the joyful excitement each day. These statements are intentionally for you to empower yourself and suggested to hold the best intention for your baby. The statements for the baby offer words of wisdom and genuine love. Sometimes both statements may resonate more for you, and others are more for the baby. All statements were written from the guidance of my heart's intuition.

The ability to maintain this connection by reading this book will create a bond that will last through eternity. Even more importantly, in the womb, we know if we are loved. Babies who are not loved grow into individuals who feel unworthy or unlovable. The subconscious mind holds on to a deep conviction of thought. Energy vibration draws to what you say. It is important to remember that there is nothing stronger than love energy. Love raises your vibrational energy.

Once the baby is born, I encourage you to reread the statements that particularly resonate with you and continue to use them. We all need a recharge or uplifting encouragement, so I truly hope that this book can make a simple difference for you.

The First Trimester

*P*regnancy is a wonderful experience but is not without a few discomforts such as morning sickness and hormonal changes. The best advice is to see your doctor early and start prenatal vitamins as soon as possible. On those days when you feel morning sickness, try to focus on anything that brings you joy. Yes, sip ginger tea or peppermint tea but focus on the baby as well. Choose to think loving thoughts of your beautiful baby and visualize what your life will be like once the baby has arrived. These simple techniques can help alleviate your discomfort. Relax and enjoy your journey. I will be with you every step of the way, and I thank you for believing.

Week 1

Day 1
Mother: "There is no greater love than the love I have for this baby."
Baby: "You are so loved."

Day 2
Mother: "I trust the process of my pregnancy."
Baby: "Trust the process of birth."

Day 3
Mother: "My baby is perfect for me."
Baby: "All is well in my eyes."

Day 4
Mother: "This baby will fill my heart with love and joy."
Baby: "You are a very important soul."

Day 5

Mother: "This baby is exactly what God/source energy has intended for me."

Baby: "The Creator connected us from this day forward."

Day 6

Mother: "I embrace the gift of this child."

Baby: "Always know that you are wanted."

Day 7

Mother: "This child, planned or not, is loved unconditionally."

Baby: "Blessing are sometimes surprises."

Week 2

Day 8

Mother: "There is no greater gift than the gift of life."

Baby: "Your precious life is a miracle."

Day 9

Mother: "Becoming pregnant and becoming a mother is a distinguishable honor and privilege."

Baby: "Honor your mother and father always and forever."

Day 10

Mother: "I am a mother and a cocreator with God/source energy."

Baby: "Thank you for allowing me the privilege of being part of this family."

Day 11

Mother: "My body is so wise. Each day it grows and expands to support a new life."

Baby: "May every cell in your body thrive and grow instinctively."

Day 12

Mother: "I honor my body, for it is strong and wise."

Baby: "You are amazingly brave."

Day 13

Mother: "All conditions are perfect for my pregnancy."

Baby: "Now is perfect timing for your development."

Day 14

Mother: "I exude an energy frequency that is positive and nurturing for my child."

Baby: "Your energy is positive and vibrant.

Week 3

Day 15

Mother: "Every day is one step closer to meeting the new life that I cocreated."

Baby: "Your day of arrival will be a joyous occasion."

Day 16

Mother: "Every cell in my body works in perfect harmony by the direction of God/source energy."

Baby: "The Creator of heaven and earth delivered you to me."

Day 17

Mother: "There is such joy in the anticipation of the new life that I bring forth into the world."

Baby: "I sing your praises, as I know you will be an amazing person."

Day 18

Mother: "Happiness and excitement resonate in every cell of my body."

Baby: "I vibe with you."

Day 19

Mother: "I firmly believe in the miracle of life."

Baby: "You are a true miracle that I love."

Day 20

Mother: "All is well in my world."

Baby: "Be who you are meant to be."

Day 21

Mother: "I practice patience today."

Baby: "You will be my teacher forevermore."

Week 4

Day 22

Mother: "I am a believer."

Baby: "Hold on to your faith and become a believer."

Day 23

Mother: "I am a wonderful cocreator."

Baby: "Create something beautiful with me."

Day 24

Mother: "I am beautiful in every way."

Baby: "You are the most beautiful soul."

Day 25

Mother: "I am a source of life to a new being."

Baby: "I will treasure your life forever."

Day 26

Mother: "I accept motherhood and flourish as I become a mother."

Baby: "I desire you to flourish and become what God intended you to be."

Day 27

Mother: "I am living a beautiful experience."

Baby: "Your existence will provide many beautiful experiences for both of us."

Day 28

Mother: "I am supported beyond my wildest dreams."

Baby: "Your dreams can come true."

Week 5

Day 29

Mother: "I greet each new experience with wonder and awe."

Baby: "I anticipate you will explore and appreciate all that is."

Day 30

Mother: "I revel in the expectation of motherhood."

Baby: "Enjoy your childhood."

Day 31

Mother: "I feel fulfilled as a woman."

Baby: "Your presence is so greatly anticipated."

Day 32

Mother: "I accept the responsibility of providing a positive atmosphere for my child to thrive."

Baby: "Your well-being is a priority in my life."

Day 33

Mother: "In this moment, I feel gratitude and appreciation for the condition of pregnancy."

Baby: "I am so grateful for your growth and development."

Day 34

Mother: "All conditions are perfect in every aspect of my pregnancy."

Baby: "It's a time to thrive and be assertive."

Day 35

Mother: "I do not have to be perfect to be the perfect parent."

Baby: "All things happen in divine timing, and you are it."

Week 6

Day 36

Mother: "I will embrace a positive attitude today."

Baby: "Your mind will develop and be creative."

Day 37

Mother: "Controlling my thoughts helps me control my emotions; therefore, I will vibe with happy thoughts."

Baby: "You will be well emotionally."

Day 38

Mother: "I support myself by thinking and feeling happy."

Baby: "Know that I will never turn my back on you."

Day 39

Mother: "Laughter brings joy within me, and my emotions are happy."

Baby: "Happiness is a gift I offer to you now."

Day 40

Mother: "Feeling happy keeps the cells in my body healthy."

Baby: "Happy baby, happy mama."

Day 41

Mother: "I accept all challenges as opportunities to learn."

Baby: "We grow together; we learn together."

Day 42

Mother: "I have joy in my heart and soul."

Baby: "This process continues to be a true soul journey."

Week 7

Day 43

Mother: "I make healthy choices for my child and me."

Baby: "Well-being is a choice."

Day 44

Mother: "I choose healthy foods to nourish my child and me."

Baby: "Together we thrive and nourish our bodies."

Day 45

Mother: "I avoid risks that affect my well-being and my body."

Baby: "Your well-being is a priority that is always on my mind."

Day 46

Mother: "I cherish every day that I am pregnant."

Baby: "Our oneness at this moment is special."

Day 47

Mother: "The transition of my body is amazing."

Baby: "Your growth is inspiring me."

Day 48

Mother: "Everything in moderation: food, exercise, and work."

Baby: "I promise to make time for us."

Day 49

Mother: "I honor my body and rest when my body feels tired."

Baby: "Rest is very important to well-being."

Week 8

Day 50

Mother: "Loving people will support my pregnancy."
Baby: "Loving people will support you in your life."

Day 51

Mother: "Helpful people are everywhere; they will assist in my pregnancy."
Baby: "Helpful people will teach, guide, and protect you in life."

Day 52

Mother: "My strength comes from my ability to believe."
Baby: "Always know you are supported from within."

Day 53

Mother: "I receive encouragement and love in miraculous ways.

Baby: "The best is yet to come."

Day 54

Mother: "My days of pregnancy are only temporary, so I appreciate them all."

Baby: "I appreciate you."

Day 55

Mother: "Sleep is important, and I will value my sleep."

Baby: "Rest well each night, for tomorrow is coming for sure."

Day 56

Mother: "I feel encouraged and appreciated by my partner."

Baby: "Your parents will always be there for you too."

Week 9

Day 57

Mother: "I will always provide for you as best as I can."

Baby: "I want you to be comfortable."

Day 58

Mother: "I will discipline with love and use the Holy Spirit as my guide."

Baby: "Keep the God/Spirit connection a priority in of your life."

Day 59

Mother: "I will teach you with love and encouragement."

Baby: "Knowledge is power, so soak it up."

Day 60

Mother: "I will take pride in your accomplishments and support your journey."

Baby: "All your achievements are acknowledged with praise."

Day 61

Mother: "I will teach my example using the power of prayer and meditation."

Baby: "Your thoughts become your reality."

Day 62

Mother: "I will be supportive in your choices."

Baby: "Truth without compassion is brutality."

Day 63

Mother: "I will take time to listen and understand your words."

Baby: "Listening is the key to communication."

Week 10

Day 64

Mother: "We will grow together as a strong family unit."

Baby: "Your value to this family is unmeasurable."

Day 65

Mother: "The bonds that connect us will be eternal."

Baby: "Our souls will never part."

Day 66

Mother: "Our lives will be enriched because we are a family."

Baby: "You are worthy."

Day 67
Mother: "We are one unit, one family, one tribe, and we embrace each other."
Baby: "Love is so powerful."

Day 68
Mother: "Together we are strong; we embrace our heritage."
Baby: "Believe that you belong here."

Day 69
Mother: "Our family is important to our community."
Baby: "You are important to this world."

Day 70
Mother: "Our family shines with love and grace."
Baby: "You are a beacon of fresh new light."

Week 11

Day 71

Mother: "Love and compassion will be the root foundation of this family."

Baby: "Nothing is stronger than the feeling of love."

Day 72

Mother: "Healthy boundaries will be respected."

Baby: "We will help you build on integrity of character."

Day 73

Mother: "Our family will play together and pray together."

Baby: "The sound of your laughter will fill our home."

Day 74

Mother: "This family is blessed in many ways."

Baby: "You are a true blessing from above."

Day 75

Mother: "Time spent together will be a joyful experience."
Baby: "Fun and excitement will be present."

Day 76

Mother: "Failure is an opportunity to stretch yourself in another direction."
Baby: "Any failure is just a moment in time to learn and move on."

Day 77

Mother: "Success is within everyone's reach."
Baby: "Your success in life is unlimited."

Week 12

Day 78

Mother: "May nature reveals its beauty to me today."

Baby: "May you see nature as it was created in beautiful splendor."

Day 79

Mother: "May I stop to smell and hear the sound of nature today."

Baby: "May you stay grounded by nature."

Day 80

Mother: "May all of nature relax my tensions."

Baby: "May you find solace with nature."

Day 81

Mother: "May my eyes be open to the wonders of nature."

Baby: "May you see nature through the same eyes as its Creator."

Day 82

Mother: "May I breathe in fresh air for my baby."

Baby: "May you enjoy the fresh air."

Day 83

Mother: "May the music I hear be beneficial to my baby."

Baby: "May you sing with a happy heart."

Day 84

Mother: "May the good vibrations of my experiences be felt by my baby."

Baby: "May you feel at peace in your surroundings."

The Second Trimester

*Y*eah! You are now in the second trimester and should have relief from some of those first trimester discomforts. You are well on your way to becoming a member of the mommy club. I want to congratulate you on your commitment to the practice of statements of truth. The small amount of time you spend on reinforcing love is so precious. There are no do-overs; it's now or never. During this phase of pregnancy, your baby can recognize touch by placing your hands on your belly. In addition, the baby recognizes your voice. The baby is developing and growing rapidly. With every day, a new developmental milestone is reached. I applaud your efforts and all the hard work you are willing to do for your beautiful baby. You are an amazing mother for trusting your intuition and using this book as a guide.

Week 13

Day 85

Mother: "I am filled with sparks of inspired ideas."
Baby: "A spark is all that is needed to begin manifesting your ideas."

Day 86

Mother: "Like a wildfire, I can ignite more creativity."
Baby: "When a spark is lit, you have unlimited possibilities."

Day 87

Mother: "The spark of sperm and my egg in perfect synchronicity created beauty."
Baby: "Your development is a beautiful miracle."

Day 88

Mother: "The spark of love between two people can manifest unlimited possibilities."

Baby: "The desire to meet you and have you in my life is amazing."

Day 89

Mother: "The spark in my life is my baby."

Baby: "I want you to know you are a bright light burning inside me."

Day 90

Mother: "The happiness I feel is coming from deep within."

Baby: "My desire is for you to feel my happiness at this moment."

Day 91

Mother: "I am connected to my inner spirit, which is a beacon of light shining."

Baby: "My hope is for you to shine your light brightly throughout your life."

Week 14

Day 92

Mother: "My choice is to be a happy mother."
Baby: "Your choices are limitless, so flow naturally to be in alignment with your path."

Day 93

Mother: "I stand in my truth as I align with God/source energy."
Baby: "The happiness you feel means you are in alignment with your path."

Day 94

Mother: "Affirmations and statements of truth are positive bursts of energy for me."
Baby: "I offer words of positive energy to guide you through your birth."

Day 95

Mother: "I am so grateful for the gift of life within my womb."

Baby: "You are a blessing I will treasure forever."

Day 96

Mother: "I am overwhelmed with delight in anticipation of your arrival."

Baby: "Understand that you are so wanted and appreciated."

Day 97

Mother: "God/Spirit is with me always."

Baby: "Believe that God/Spirit is with you always."

Day 98

Mother: "I am well today because I am alive."

Baby: "I believe you will love your life."

Week 15

Day 99

Mother: "I feel guided by Spirit today."

Baby: "Continue to seek spirituality through life."

Day 100

Mother: "I enjoy learning, and books are full of knowledge."

Baby: "Continue to read and never stop learning."

Day 101

Mother: "I listen with an open heart."

Baby: "'Continue to listen intently."

Day 102

Mother: "I value my life and those of others."

Baby: "Continue to value yourself."

Day 103

Mother: "I trust my feelings."

Baby: "Continue to trust your instincts."

Day 104

Mother: "I am so grateful."

Baby: "Continue to receive with a grateful heart."

Day 105

Mother: "I pray and meditate to strengthen myself."

Baby: "Continue to pray and meditate."

Week 16

Day 106

Mother: "I pray your angels watch over you from your first breath until your last breath."

Baby: "Listen to your inner voice."

Day 107

Mother: "I pray you learn by experiencing life lessons and grow with each lesson."

Baby: "Live life for the experiences."

Day 108

Mother: "I pray you learn that giving is the key to expanding your heart."

Baby: "Give generously."

Day 109

Mother: "I pray for your safety."

Baby: "Use caution and your intuition."

Day 110

Mother: "I pray you have a blessed life."

Baby: "You always get what you vibrationally are."

Day 111

Mother: "I pray you reach your full potential."

Baby: "You become what you believe and know."

Day 112

Mother: "I will pray every day for you, now and through eternity."

Baby: "Your soul is your compass."

Week 17

Day 113

Mother: "My child will navigate well in contrasting situations."

Baby: "Avoid negative people; they will add no value to your life."

Day 114

Mother: "My child comes from a place of peace and love."

Baby: "Walk in peace and love as much as possible."

Day 115

Mother: "My child radiates health and wellness."

Baby: "Your choices will predict your health and wellness."

Day 116

Mother: "My child understands spiritual vibrations."

Baby: "Be aware of the spiritual lessons in life."

Day 117

Mother: "My child is fearless because he or she walks with faith."

Baby: "God/spiritual energy is bigger than human imagination."

Day 118

Mother: "My child wants to live in peace."

Baby: "Through peace, the world can change."

Day 119

Mother: "My child will inspire others to do their best."

Baby: "Always choose to uplift because, for it will bring out a better outcome."

Week 18

Day 120

Mother: "This child is ready to thrive and prosper."

Baby: "The world is awaiting your arrival."

Day 121

Mother: "This child is inspired to achieve great things."

Baby: "Inspiration comes from divine source energy/God.

Day 122

Mother: "This child is full of potential."

Baby: "Know that your opportunities begin with your desire."

Day 123

Mother: "This child is going to bring joy to the world."

Baby: "Just be happy and your light will shine."

Day 124

Mother: "This child will not give up easily."

Baby: "Challenges will be fun to overcome."

Day 125

Mother: "This child has great purpose to my life."

Baby: "Nothing is done by accident."

Day 126

Mother: "This child is capable of loving deeply."

Baby: "Love is so powerful."

Week 19

Day 127

Mother: "I focus on positive thoughts only."
Baby: "You receive the energy with which you surround yourself."

Day 128

Mother: "I am a role model for my child."
Baby: "Follow those with integrity from the heart."

Day 129

Mother: "I demonstrate faith and live it."
Baby: "Search for the truth and there you will find your answers."

Day 130

Mother: "I live with joy in my heart."

Baby: "There is no better way to live than with a heart and soul full of joy."

Day 131

Mother: "I relish my relationship with this child."

Baby: "Respect and admiration are mutual."

Day 132

Mother: "I enjoy every moment of every day."

Baby: "Life is meant to be lived with ease."

Day 133

Mother: "I love my life."

Baby: "Life is precious—so love it."

Week 20

Day 134

Mother: "Unexpected gifts show up for me."
Baby: "Live in expectancy and you will never be disappointed."

Day 135

Mother: "I am thankful for every gift; big and small, I receive them all."
Baby: "Give thanks always."

Day 136

Mother: "I can manifest my heart's desires."
Baby: "Your thoughts create your reality."

Day 137

Mother: "My power is my love."

Baby: "There is no greater power than the power of *love*."

Day 138

Mother: "I am in alignment of expectation."

Baby: "A balanced life is a life of true alignment."

Day 139

Mother: "I choose to live a life of peace."

Baby: "A peaceful life is a comfortable life."

Day 140

Mother: "My body is in the rhythm of pregnancy."

Baby: "Respect your body and be kind to yourself."

Week 21

Day 141

Mother: "Your family is the first tribe you will belong to."

Baby: "You can join many clubs, groups, and associations, but family was first."

Day 142

Mother: "I welcome family traditions and invoke new ones."

Baby: "Embrace what is and embrace what can be."

Day 143

Mother: "Use your inner guidance to stay balanced."

Baby: "Rely on what you feel as your compass."

Day 144

Mother: "Focus on the goodness of your life today."

Baby: "Wake up thinking, *What is good in my life today?*"

Day 145

Mother: "Be aware of what you are doing."

Baby: "Stay present in the moment."

Day 146

Mother: "Notice how life just unfolds when you are enjoying life."

Baby: "Give and you will receive."

Day 147

Mother: "Notice that you attract what you want when the desire is strong."

Baby: "Desire is a strong magnet to what you want. Use it wisely!"

Week 22

Day 148

Mother: "Today I choose kindness in all that I do."
Baby: "Being kind opens all kinds of doors."

Day 149

Mother: "Today I choose compassion in all that I do."
Baby: "A tear of compassion changes everything."

Day 150

Mother: "Today I choose to follow the path that is mine."
Baby: "Honor your journey."

Day 151

Mother: "Today I choose God/universal energy to give me strength."

Baby: "Draw from the well of endless supply—God/universal source energy."

Day 152

Mother: "Today I choose what makes me feel good in any situation."

Baby: "You always have a choice."

Day 153

Mother: "Today I choose to see the sweetness in everyday life."

Baby: "Simplicity feels good."

Day 154

Mother: "Today I choose to respond and not react."

Baby: "Slow down and just breathe."

Week 23

Day 155

Mother: "Lessons in life allow me to be the person who I am."

Baby: "I am who I am."

Day 156

Mother: "Repeating the same life lessons means I must become aware and wake up."

Baby: "Let go when things get stuck in your life."

Day 157

Mother: "Trying something without positive energy effort has no value."

Baby: "Resistance is built-up negative energy."

Day 158

Mother: "Giving openly from your heart is most rewarding."

Baby: "Feel the joy of an open heart."

Day 159

Mother: "Your inner guidance system is your clear connection to all that is."

Baby: "Intuition is a mechanism, like a GPS."

Day 160

Mother: "Today I feel such peace and harmony."

Baby: "Soak up energy vibrations of peace and harmony."

Day 161

Mother: "Release what doesn't serve you because it is toxic to your well-being."

Baby: "Being well is the same as well-being."

Week 24

Day 162

Mother: "Allow anger to pass through you, but don't hold on to it."

Baby: "Let the energy flow like a river."

Day 163

Mother: "Be filled with happiness and flow with ease."

Baby: "Every day is a new day to reset and begin anew."

Day 164

Mother: "Our memories are snapshots of our lifetime."

Baby: "Create memories; they last a lifetime."

Day 165

Mother: "Take mental pictures; they will be with you always."

Baby: "Stop and smell the roses."

Day 166

Mother: "Your imagination is limitless."

Baby: "All that you imagine is from God/universal energy."

Day 167

Mother: "Fill your mind with positive thoughts when you go to bed and wake up."

Baby: "Big ideas come to those who can imagine them."

Day 168

Mother: "Uplift others to enhance your well-being."

Baby: "Doing for others fills you with good feelings."

Week 25

Day 169

Mother: "Learn to live with a happy heart."

Baby: "A happy heart is a choice."

Day 170

Mother: "Learn the art of forgiving."

Baby: "In forgiveness, you receive freedom."

Day 171

Mother: "Learn to place trust in yourself."

Baby: "Trusting yourself is enabling power."

Day 172

Mother: "Learn to seek joy in your work."

Baby: "Your work should be fulfilling."

Day 173

Mother: "Learn to listen before you respond."

Baby: "Understanding is the key to communication."

Day 174

Mother: "Learn to keep expanding your mind."

Baby: "It is the responsibility of all human being to expand themselves."

Day 175

Mother: "Learn to appreciate and be grateful."

Baby: "It is fun to find appreciation in every day."

Week 26

Day 176

Mother: "Mind your own business."

Baby: "Stay on your path; everyone has their own journey."

Day 177

Mother: "Stay true to yourself."

Baby: "Be you."

Day 178

Mother: "Your best is good enough."

Baby: "Everyone is blessed in many ways so just do your personal best."

Day 179
Mother: "Take notice of all the beautiful things around you."
Baby: "Look at beautiful things and appreciate them."

Day 180
Mother: "Feed your soul."
Baby: "Appreciation, gratitude, forgiveness, alignment, and truth are essential."

Day 181
Mother: "Be a ray of sunshine to everyone."
Baby: "Smile big."

Day 182
Mother: "Pray for peace; it is everyone's duty."
Baby: "Prayer works; don't give up."

Week 27

Day 183
Mother: "Live with love and joy in your heart."
Baby: "Yes, for a happy heart has a beautiful life."

Day 184
Mother: "Dare to care about our world."
Baby: "Bridge the gap with compassion and understanding."

Day 185
Mother: "Happiness comes from within."
Baby: "Be kind to yourself and others."

Day 186
Mother: "Spend quiet time with your thoughts."
Baby: "Meditation and prayer reset your mind."

Day 187

Mother: "Have the courage to speak up."

Baby: "Use your voice or position to support those with no voice."

Day 188

Mother: "Honor your feelings."

Baby: "Your feelings matter."

Day 189

Mother: "Where you are now is not the end; it may just be a resting point in life."

Baby: "Struggle is real; look at that contrast to self-correct."

The Third Trimester

I am so very excited for you because you have reached the third trimester. It is natural to gain weight and feel big. Now is the time to take action to prepare for childbirth. I suggest walking as your exercise, for it has many health benefits and is a way to connect with nature. Walking outdoors would be ideal, but if it's too cold to walk outside, try a treadmill or walk at a mall. Walking helps the baby drop into place and provides good blood flow circulation. As you walk, you can easily meditate and think about your statement of truth. This is just another suggestion as to how you can use the book. Most importantly, find a time that best fits your schedule and enjoy the process.

In a few weeks, you will be delivering a beautiful baby, and I just want to say how much I appreciate our connecting along the way. I may not be your mother, sister, or dear friend, but I am a member of the mommy group and do consider you a woman connected through sisterhood. I want you to remain calm and think about all your favorite statement of truth when going into delivery. Remember to focus on what you want and make that your priority. I wish the best for you and your baby.

Week 28

Day 190

Mother: "You are never stuck in a situation. If you prefer something else, then move."

Baby: "Water will flow around a rock in the middle of a stream, so float and go with the flow."

Day 191

Mother: "Emotions and feelings are your internal guidance system."

Baby: "Notice how you feel before you make a decision."

Day 192

Mother: "Emotions can be controlled by you."

Baby: "Emotions are a result of how you are feeling."

Day 193

Mother: "You feel best when your emotions are balanced."

Baby: "Meditation is a good way to get centered."

Day 194

Mother: "Quiet your mind and feel what your emotions are saying."

Baby: "Prayer is a good way to find peace of mind."

Day 195

Mother: "Notice how clear you become when your mind is quiet."

Baby: "Consciousness speaks to a quiet mind."

Day 196

Mother: "Inspiration from a quiet mind is God speaking to you."

Baby: "Listen to your inner voice."

Week 29

Day 197

Mother: "Forgiveness is not weakness; it is where you get strength."

Baby: "Forgiveness is an act of kindness."

Day 198

Mother: "Forgiveness is an opportunity to release all that doesn't serve you."

Baby: "Release all judgment."

Day 199

Mother: "Forgiveness is the ultimate act of kindness to yourself."

Baby: "Allow yourself to forgive."

Day 200

Mother: "Forgiveness is a way to release all resistance."

Baby: "Resistance blocks the flow of good energy."

Day 201

Mother: "Forgiveness is the key to free the soul."

Baby: "Allow your soul to live freely."

Day 202

Mother: "Through forgiveness, you strengthen your own faith."

Baby: "Believe in what gives you a happy life."

Day 203

Mother: "Forgiveness opens your heart and feels good."

Baby: "Good things come to those who feel good."

Week 30

Day 204

Mother: "Challenge is an opportunity to grow."

Baby: "Challenge yourself, not others."

Day 205

Mother: "I'm doing my best with what I have."

Baby: "You don't have to complete against anyone; your best is good enough."

Day 206

Mother: "I hunger for healthy foods."

Baby: "Eat healthy to be healthy."

Day 207

Mother: "My body is changing to prepare for birth."

Baby: "Change is hard; be flexible."

Day 208

Mother: "Anything I set my mind to can happen."

Baby: "Aim high; goals are attainable."

Day 209

Mother: "Everything I ever needed is within me."

Baby: "Rise above the crowd to see opportunities."

Day 210

Mother: "It is my desire to provide a safe, healthy, and happy home."

Baby: "You must desire to excel."

Week 31

Day 211

Mother: "I pray your angels watch over you from your first breath until your last breath."

Baby: "Feel the power of faith."

Day 212

Mother: "I pray you learn by experiencing life lessons and grow with each lesson."

Baby: "Rise above your raising."

Day 213

Mother: "I pray you learn that giving is the key to expanding your heart."

Baby: "Be compassionate with yourself and others."

Day 214

Mother: "I pray you learn to appreciate all of nature."

Baby: "Appreciation wipes out any feeling of lack."

Day 215

Mother: "I pray you can be strong and healthy."

Baby: "Your body is the human shield that protects your heart and soul."

Day 216

Mother: "I pray you understand respect and use it."

Baby: "Respect is a two-way street; you must earn it to receive it. You must give it to know it."

Day 217

Mother: "I pray your heart and soul are filled with love."

Baby: "Love is your superpower."

Week 32

Day 218

Mother: "I feel your love before I even meet you."

Baby: "Love radiates from within."

Day 219

Mother: "Knowing you are my child is expanding my own light."

Baby: "Love is equivalent to light."

Day 220

Mother: "I love you, sweet baby."

Baby: "Love flows from within."

Day 221

Mother: "Love promotes wellness."

Baby: "Love can cure illness."

Day 222

Mother: "In our home, love will always win."

Baby: "Love is stronger than hate."

Day 223

Mother: "All discipline will be out of love."

Baby: "Love conquers conflict."

Day 224

Mother: "I have an endless supply of love to give you."

Baby: "Love is shared, not withheld."

Week 33

Day 225

Mother: "I am grateful for all my talents."

Baby: "Talent is your gift from God."

Day 226

Mother: "I look forward to watching you evolve over the years."

Baby: "Everyone has a beautiful talent."

Day 227

Mother: "Conquer your fears by facing them."

Baby: "Fears and phobias are stories made up and believed to be true by you but actually are not true.

Day 228

Mother: "Today I practice gratitude in all that I do."

Baby: "Gratitude is a feeling of deep thankfulness."

Day 229

Mother: "My decisions and actions are from my experiences."

Baby: "Intelligence is understanding an idea or concept."

Day 230

Mother: "Law of attraction: you receive what you are a match to."

Baby: "Resistance blocks the good that wants to come to you."

Day 231

Mother: "Today I will appreciate more."

Baby: "Appreciation is in alignment with God/Spirit and the universe.

Week 34

Day 232
Mother: "My fulfillment is from my own actions."
Baby: "May your life be interesting for you."

Day 233
Mother: "Hope gives me something to look forward to."
Baby: "May your dreams be big."

Day 234
Mother: "May our lives complement each other."
Baby: "May your days be filled with happiness."

Day 235
Mother: "I will do my best to look for the best in every situation."
Baby: "May your attitude be positive."

Day 236

Mother: "Today I will smile a lot."

Baby: "May your smile be bright."

Day 237

Mother: "I am filled with enthusiasm as this pregnancy is nearing the end."

Baby: "May your energy be magnetic."

Day 238

Mother: "My hands are here to hold, guide, and balance you."

Baby: "May your hands be helpful."

Week 35

Day 239
Mother: "Encouragement uplifts."
Baby: "Mistakes are not failures."

Day 240
Mother: "Uplifting spreads joy."
Baby: "Failures are ways to learn."

Day 241
Mother: "Joy is exuberant happiness."
Baby: "Learning provides insight."

Day 242
Mother: "Happiness leads to success."
Baby: "Insight develops new ideas."

Day 243

Mother: "Success needs nurturing."

Baby: "New ideas promote growth."

Day 244

Mother: "Nurturing feeds believing in something."

Baby: "Growth expands minds."

Day 245

Mother: "Believe it to achieve it."

Baby: "Expanded minds produce peace, harmony, and love."

Week 36

Day 246

Mother: "I start this day with wonder and awe."

Baby: "Remember that every day is a new beginning."

Day 247

Mother: "Do what's right and you will never be wrong."

Baby: "Remember that you always have a choice."

Day 248

Mother: "I am so loved."

Baby: "Remember that God always loves you."

Day 249

Mother: "Parenting is a human experience I chose."

Baby: "Remember that parents are not perfect."

Day 250

Mother: "Meditation/prayer is my go-to."

Baby: "Remember to stay in alignment and remain balanced in life."

Day 251

Mother: "I will stay focused on the present and leave worry behind."

Baby: "Remember to focus on the now; be aware of your feelings."

Day 252

Mother: "I take responsibility about how I feel."

Baby: "Remember to live joyfully."

Week 37

Day 253
Mother: "My intuition is my compass in all that I do."
Baby: "Trust yourself always."

Day 254
Mother: "My wisdom comes from experiences."
Baby: "Be mindful in all that you do."

Day 255
Mother: "In days of doubt, I pray and/or meditate."
Baby: "Call on God/Spirit, for he is near."

Day 256
Mother: "My strength is in my faith."
Baby: "Faith doesn't have to be a religion."

Day 257

Mother: "My hope is in my beliefs."

Baby: "Never stop hoping."

Day 258

Mother: "My thoughts create my reality."

Baby: "Be as creative as you want."

Day 259

Mother: "My courage brings me closer to my destiny."

Baby: "Allow yourself to receive the goodness of the universe."

Week 38

Day 267

Mother: "With every breath I take, I breathe in peace and breathe out love."

Baby: "Fulfillment of oneself is yours; just breathe."

Day 268

Mother: "I will remain calm and trust the process as my body prepares for birth."

Baby: "Your arrival will be divine timing."

Day 269

Mother: "Love is the most powerful feeling."

Baby: "You have grown nine months in a body of love."

Day 270
Mother: "May the conditions within my womb allow this baby to thrive."
Baby: "Your arrival is with great pleasure."

Day 271
Mother: "My body is in the rhythm of pregnancy."
Baby: "We will do this delivery together."

Day 272
Mother: "I embrace the beautiful changes to my body."
Baby: "You are a beautiful person."

Day 273
Mother: "Motherhood is my sisterhood."
Baby: "Welcome to this world."

Week 39

Day 274
Mother: "Each day is full of excitement as I near the delivery of my baby."
Baby: "Be excited, for your day is coming soon."

Day 275
Mother: "I will deliver with ease."
Baby: "Go with the flow."

Day 276
Mother: "I see my delivery as a beautiful experience."
Baby: "Mama's arms are waiting my arrival."

Day 277

Mother: "I will focus on statements of truth during my delivery."

Baby: "Remember to just breathe."

Day 278

Mother: "My body knows how to prepare for delivery."

Baby: "Your body is ready for birth."

Day 279

Mother: "Each delivery is different yet special in its own way."

Baby: "Now is the perfect timing for your entrance into this world."

Day 280

Mother: "Every woman experiences some degree of pain, but I will embrace the experience with positive affirmations."

Baby: "The purest form of love and innocence are now released."

Spark

The joy I felt when I found out I was pregnant was nothing short of exuberant excitement. The joy I felt when I birthed my first son was over the moon ecstatic *love*. I am sure if you have given birth, you were feeling those emotions too. This is the spark of love. You do not realize the amount of love that can pour out of your human heart until you birth your own baby. Now it is time to utilize the words and patience you have practiced.

You have the power to influence your own subconscious mind and through it gain the cooperation of infinite intelligence or God's grace. However you view this is your prerogative. Knowledge is your potential power. Your connection to your inner truth will guide you and inspire you to parent with love. Lead with love by choosing what is a balanced life for you. You will know it is balanced because you flow with ease and grace and everything just falls into place perfectly. What is balanced for you may not be the same for someone else, so don't compare yourself to anyone. Be true to you; there is no competition in raising a family. I believe the only benefit in competition is knowing what you really want. It always becomes crystal clear when you follow your heart's desire.

Once you have launched the trajectory of your desires and begun focusing on positive affirmations, it easily becomes your habit to choose harmony, which will enrich your life positively in every choice that you make. This is not just practice, but living in harmony is your choice. You have the power within you to allow your mind and emotions to be loving and compassionate and nurturing or anxious and out of alignment when parenting your child. This baby will grow very quickly and mirror your behavior; children are a direct product of the environment they live in. This is why from the very beginning of this child's birth, take time to work on you so that you can be the best parent to your child. One small step every day will lead to many big results. You are not alone, and women all over the world struggle with the same anxieties: am I doing this right? Simply allow your instinct to parent from a loving heart and you will never fail. I have one statement of truth I will share with you now, which I used in the beginning of my work, and it goes like this: "When prayer and meditation become your habit, miracles will become your lifestyle." I love the power of these words. It brings a good feeling that good things are going to happen for me.

Nothing is more satisfying and fulfilling than to raise a child who is well behaved and a joy to be around. Integrity, character, and self-control are morals that a mother can encourage early on. When women support each other, incredible things can happen. This is why I am writing this book. Now is the time to turn the tide and bring basic moral principles back to society. Learning begins at birth and continues through the rest of life. Good manners can be achieved by anyone from any economical or geographical stature. Religious or nonreligious differences make no difference to the contributions of human well-being. All people deserve to be treated with respect. Women, you have the power to create and end what no longer serves the greater good for humanity.

Your child is like a garden: you can plant seeds of love and compassion or fear and hate. You can ignore it and allow weeds to take over or you can water it and tend to it, which will reap far more deliciousness then you could ever imagine. This parenting is the single most important duty that you will ever do in your entire life, and it can get tough at times. The pains and the hard work can also bring unmeasurable joy to your life. However, remember that you are the one bringing a human life into existence out of the spark of a single desire.

My dream was to write a book to help inspire others to use the power of love energy in a new way. I was inspired to start this first book at the beginning, where life initially begins at conception. Out of that *spark* comes forth a human being. I am often asked to speak about energy and its power behind our words. The previous statements are very powerful because the intention is offered as heartfelt love energy. I wanted to help mothers understand that their words and thoughts carry powerful emotions that babies can feel and carry in their subconscious state of mind for the rest of their lives. I try my best to be an uplifting person and to share encouragement with others as guideposts for manifesting. Congratulations on the birth of your child/children and enjoy the journey.

I wish you love, peace, and joy forevermore.

Printed in the United States
By Bookmasters